香港國際詩歌之夜 2017
INTERNATIONAL POETRY NIGHTS IN HONG KONG

編輯 Editors

北島 Bei Dao

柯夏智 Lucas Klein

宋子江 Chris Song

養鶴問題

陳先發

THE QUESTION OF RAISING CRANES

CHEN XIANFA

《養鶴問題》
陳先發 著

封面影像：北島

國際統一書號（ISBN）：978-988-237-032-6

出版：中文大學出版社
香港 新界 沙田・香港中文大學
傳真：+852 2603 7355
電郵：cup@cuhk.edu.hk
網址：www.chineseupress.com

The Question of Raising Cranes
By Chen Xianfa

Cover Image: Bei Dao

ISBN: 978-988-237-032-6

Published by The Chinese University Press
The Chinese University of Hong Kong
Sha Tin, N.T., Hong Kong
Fax: +852 2603 7355
E-mail: cup@cuhk.edu.hk
Website: www.chineseupress.com

Printed in Hong Kong

目錄 Contents

丹青見 8
Seen in a Painting

前世 10
A Past Life

從達摩到慧能的邏輯學研究 12
The Study of Logic from Dharma to Hui-Neng

菠菜帖 14
A Post on Spinach

養鶴問題 18
The Question of Raising Cranes

夜間的一切 21
Everything at Night

憶顧准 25
Remembering Gu Zhun

泡沫簡史 31
Brief Chronicle of Bubbles

崖邊口占 34
Cliffside Account

枯樹賦 36
Ode to a Withered Tree

街頭即繪 40
Improvised Street Painting

渺茫的本體 42
The Unspeakable Body

歲聿其逝 46
A Year in Passing

不可多得的容器 48
Rare Containers

深嗅 50
Deep Sniffing

在永失中 54
In Eternal Loss

膝上牡丹花 58
The Peonies on the Knees

陳先發
Chen Xianfa

English translation by Tammy Ho Lai-Ming

丹青見

檀木，白松，榆樹和水杉，高於接骨木，紫荊
鐵皮桂和香樟。湖水被秋天挽著向上，針葉林高於
闊葉林，野杜仲高於亂蓬蓬的劍麻。如果
湖水暗漲，柞木將高於紫檀。鳥鳴，一聲接一聲地
溶化著。蛇的舌頭如受電擊，她從鎖眼中窺見的樺樹
高於從旋轉著的玻璃中，窺見的樺樹。
死人眼中的樺樹，高於生者眼中的樺樹。
被製成棺木的樺樹，高於被製成提琴的樺樹。

2004 年10 月

Seen in a Painting

Alder, white pine, elm, and metasequoia are taller than
elderberry, bauhinia, tin tree, and camphor. Autumn drags
lake water up, and coniferous forests are higher
than broadleaf, wild eucommia than messy sisal. If water
rises in secret, oak will overtop sandalwood. One after the
other, bird calls
melt. The snake tongue looks electrocuted, as the birch she
spies from locked eyes
is taller than the birch spied in rotating glass.
Birch in the dead's eyes is taller than birch in living eyes.
The birch made into a coffin is higher than birch made
into a violin.

October 2004

前世

要逃，就乾脆逃到蝴蝶的體內去
不必再咬著牙，打翻父母的陰謀和藥汁
不必等到血都吐盡了。
要為敵，就乾脆與整個人類為敵。
他嘩地一下脱掉了蘸墨的青袍
脱掉了一層皮
脱掉了內心朝飛暮倦的長亭短亭。
脱掉了雲和水
這情節確實令人震悚：他如此輕易地
又脱掉了自己的骨頭！
我無限眷戀的最後一幕是：他們縱身一躍
在枝頭等了億年的蝴蝶渾身一顫
暗叫道：來了！
這一夜明月低於屋檐
碧溪潮生兩岸

只有一句尚未忘記
她忍住百感交集的淚水
把左翅朝下壓了壓，往前一伸
說：梁兄，請了
請了——

2004 年6 月2 日

A Past Life

To escape, simply retreat into a butterfly's body
no need to clench your teeth or overturn parental plans and elixirs
no need to wait till you've spat out all your blood.
To make enemies, let it be against all humanity.
With a huff, he strips off his ink-stained robe
shedding his own skin
shedding his heart's dawn-dusk darting from long pavilions and
  short pavilions
shedding clouds and water
It *is* a shocking scene: so easily
he tears off his own bones again!
The final scene that lingers in my mind: they leap
and the butterflies waiting on the branch for a million years
  flutter their wings
quietly beckoning: Come!
This night the moon is lower than the eaves
Two shores grow out of the turquoise tide

Only one sentence is not forgotten
She withholds tears of a hundred emotions
presses down her left wing, then stretches forward
to say, Brother Liang, Farewell
Farewell—Farewell—

2 June 2004

從達摩到慧能的邏輯學研究

面壁者坐在一把尺子
和一堵牆
之間
他向哪邊移動一點，哪邊的木頭
就會裂開

（假設這尺子是相對的
又掉下來，很難開口）

為了破壁他生得醜
為了破壁他種下了
兩畦青菜

2005 年1月

The Study of Logic from Dharma to Hui-Neng

Facing the wall he sits between a ruler
and a wall
in whichever direction he moves, the wood
splits

(Assuming that this ruler is relative
and falls, which is hard to say)

To break open the wall he was born ugly
to break open the wall he planted
two plots of vegetables

January 2005

菠菜帖

母親從鄉下捎來菠菜一捆
根上帶著泥土
這泥土，被我視作禮物的一部分。
也是將要剔除的一部分：
——在鄉村，泥土有
更多的用途
可用於自殺，也可用來堵住滾燙的喉嚨

甚至可以用來猜謎。
南方丘陵常見的紅壤，雨水
從中間剝離出砂粒
母親仍喜歡在那上面勞作。
它又將長出甚麼？
我猜得中的終將消失。
我猜不到的，將統治這個亂糟糟的世界

是誰說過「事物之外、別無思想」？
一首詩的荒謬正在於
它變幻不定的容器
藏不住這一捆不能言說的菠菜。
它的青色幾乎是

一種抵制——
母親知道我對世界有著太久的怒氣

我轉身打電話對母親說：
「太好吃了」。
「有一種剛出獄的澀味」。
我能看見她在晚餐中的
獨飲
菠菜在小酒杯中又將成熟
而這個傍晚將依賴更深的泥土燃盡。
我對匱乏的渴求勝於被填飽的渴求

2012年1月

A Post on Spinach

Mother picked spinach and brought it back from her village
earth still clinging to its roots
I saw this earth as part of the gift.
But it is also a part to be expunged:
—in the village, earth has
many functions
it can be used for suicide, or to stuff a burning throat

It could even be used to guess a riddle
the red soil seen in the Southern hills, raindrops
with sand grains stripped from their core
Mother still likes to labour on it.
What will it grow into?
What I can guess will disappear.
What I can't guess will take control of this chaotic world

Who said "No ideas but in things"?
The absurdity of a poem lies in
its inconstant vessel
which cannot contain this mute clump of spinach.
Its green is almost

a kind of resistance—
Mother knows I hold grudges against the world too long

I give her a call:
"This is so delicious."
"It tastes acerbic, like it's just out of jail."
I can picture her at dinner
drinking alone
And the spinach in the small wine glass ripening
as dusk depends on the ignition of a deeper vein of loam.
My thirst to be filled yields to my thirst for scarcity

January 2012

養鶴問題

在山中，我見過柱狀的鶴。
液態的、或氣體的鶴。
在肅穆的杜鵑花根部蜷成一團春泥的鶴。
都緩緩地斂起翅膀。
我見過這唯一為虛構而生的飛禽
因她的白色飽含了拒絕，而在
這末世，長出了更合理的形體

養鶴是垂死者才能玩下去的遊戲。
同為少數人的宗教，寫詩
卻是另一碼事：
這結句裏的「鶴」完全可以被代替。
永不要問，代它到這世上一哭的是些甚麼事物。
當它哭著東，也哭著西。
哭著密室政治，也哭著街頭政治。
就像今夜，在浴室排風機的轟鳴裏
我久久地坐著
彷彿永不會離開這裏一步。
我是個不曾養鶴也不曾殺鶴的俗人。
我知道時代賦予我的痛苦已結束了。
我披著純白的浴衣，
從一個批判者正大踏步地趕至旁觀者的位置上。

2012 年4 月

The Question of Raising Cranes

In the mountains, I have seen pillar-shaped cranes.
In liquid form, or in vapour.
At the roots of solemn azaleas, cranes ball themselves
into mud.
They languidly gather their wings.
I have seen this bird, which exists only for fiction,
taking a more reasonable shape in these end times,
because its white engulfs refusal

Raising cranes is a game for dying men.
Also a minority religion, though writing poetry
is another matter:
The "cranes" in that line can totally be replaced.
Don't ever ask, *what will replace its crying in this world.*
When it's crying for this, it's crying for that.
It cries for politics in the corridors, and cries for the
politics of the street.
Like tonight, surrounded by the sounds from the bathroom
exhaust fan
I sit for a long time on the floor
as if I'd never leave one step away.

I am a layperson who has never raised or killed a crane.
I know the suffering this age has bestowed on me has
ended.
I put on a pristine white bathrobe,
and in sweeping steps, switch from critic to onlooker.

April 2012

夜間的一切

我時常覺得自己枯竭了。正如此刻
一家人圍著桌子分食的菠蘿——

菠蘿轉眼就消失了。
而我們的嘴唇仍在半空中，吮吸著

母親就坐在桌子那邊。父親死後她幾近失明
在夜裏，點燃灰白的頭撞著牆壁

我們從不同的世界伸出舌頭。但我永不知道
菠蘿在她牙齒上裂出甚麼樣的味道

就像幼時的遊戲中我們永不知她藏身何處。
在櫃子裏找她
在鐘擺上找她
在淅淅瀝瀝滴著雨的葵葉的背面找她
事實上，她藏在一支舊鋼筆中等著我們前去擰開。沒人知道，
連她自己也不知道

但夜間的一切盡可刪除
包括白熾燈下這場對飲

我們像菠蘿一樣被切開，離去
像杯子一樣深深地碰上
嗅著對方，又被走廊盡頭甚麼東西撞著牆壁的
「咚、咚、咚」的聲音永恆地隔開

2012 年 9 月

Everything at Night

I often find myself withering. Like this moment
with my family around the table dividing a pineapple—

the pineapple is soon gone.
And our mouths are in mid-air, sucking

Mother sits at the far end of the table, near-blind since
father died.
At night, she bangs her ash-white head on the wall.

We stick our tongues out from different worlds. But I
never know
the taste of pineapple split in her teeth

Like our childhood game when we never knew where
she was hiding.
Looking for her in the cupboard
Looking for her in the swinging clock
Looking for her behind the sunflower leaves dripping rain

In fact, she was hiding in an old fountain pen waiting for
us to unscrew its cap. Nobody knew.
Not even herself

But everything at night can be struck out,
including the one-on-one drinking beneath this white lamp.
We are cut open like the pineapple, and leave
like glasses clinking heartily
sniffing each other, but also separated forever like some
nameless thing
thudding at the end of the corridor.

September 2012

憶顧准

讓他酷刑中的眼光投向我們。
穿過病房、圍牆、鐵絲網和
真理被過度消耗的稀薄空氣中
仍開得璀璨的白色夾竹桃花。
他不會想到，
有人將以詩歌來殘忍地談論這一切。
我們相隔39年。
他死去，只為了剩下我們

這是一個以充分蹂躪換取
充分懷疑的時代。
就像此刻，我讀著文革時期史料
脖子上總有剃刀掠過的沁涼。
屋內一切都如此可疑：
舊檯燈裏藏著密信？
地上繩子，彷彿隨時直立起來
擰成絞索，
將我吊死。
如果我呼救，圓月將從窗口撲進來堵我的嘴

逃到公園
每一角落都有隱形人
衝出來向我問好

要麼像老舍那樣投身湖下，
頭頂幾片枯荷下下棋、聽聽琴？
可劊子手
也喜歡到水下踱步。
制度從不饒恕任何一個激進的地址。

1974年，這個火熱的人死於國家對他的拒絕
或者，正相反——
用細節複述一具肉身的離去已毫無意義。
1975年，當河南板橋水庫垮壩
瞬間到來的24萬冤魂
願意舉著燈為他的話作出注釋。
我常想
最純粹的鏡像僅能在污穢中生成，而
當世只配享有傑克遜那樣的病態天才。
憶顧准，
是否意味著我一樣的沉屙在身？

但我已學會了從遮蔽中捕獲微妙的營養。
説起來這也不算啥稀奇的事兒
我所求不多
只願一碗稀粥伴我至晚年
粥中漂著的三、兩個孤魂也伴我至晚年

2013年3月18日

Remembering Gu Zhun

Let his tortured eyes cast upon us.
Through hospital wards, walls, wire fences, and
truth resplendent white oleanders can still bloom
in the over-consumed thin air.
He'd never have thought
Someone would cruelly discuss all this in a poem.
We have been separated 39 years.
He died, to leave us behind.

This is a time when full savagery replaces
full suspicion.
Like now, reading documents of the Cultural Revolution,
the razor's cold glide is always at my neck.
Everything in the house is so suspicious:
A confidential letter in the old desk lamp?
The rope on the floor about to rise up
into a noose,
And hang me.
If I scream, the full moon will leap through the window
to cork my mouth.

Escape into the park,
Where invisible men from every corner
Accost me to ask how I am

Perhaps it's better to jump into a lake like Lao She,
To play chess and heed the zither beneath the lily pads?
But those executioners
Also like taking walks in the water.
The system allows no radical address.

In 1974, this fiery person died in the country's rejection
Or perhaps it's the opposite—
Meticulous description of the corporeal body's departure
  is meaningless.
In 1975, when the Banqiao Dam in Henan collapsed
Two hundred and forty thousand innocent ghosts
  suddenly appeared
To hold up lanterns, annotating his words.
I often think
The purest image can only grow from filth, but

This generation only deserves the squalid genius of a
Jackson Pollock.
Does remembering Gu Zhun
Mean that I have a lingering illness, too?

But I've learnt to gain a subtle nutrition from hiding.
It's really not that remarkable.
I don't ask for much:
A thin bowl of gruel to accompany me in old age
With a couple lonely ghosts or three drifting in it.

18 March 2013

泡沫簡史

熾烈人世炙我如炭
也贈我小片陰翳清涼如斯
我未曾像薇依和僧璨那樣以苦行
來醫治人生的斷裂
我沒有蒸沙作飯的胃口
也尚未產生割肉伺虎的膽氣
我生於萬木清新的河岸
是一排排泡沫
來敲我的門
我知道前仆後繼的死
必須讓位於這爭分奪秒的破裂
暮晚的河面，流漩相接
我看著無邊的泡沫破裂
在它們破裂並恢復為流水之前
有一種神秘力量尚未命名
彷彿思想的怪物正
無依無靠地隱身其中
我知道把一個個語言與意志的
破裂連接起來舞動
乃是我終生的工作
必須惜己如螻蟻
我的大廈正建築在空空如也的泡沫上

2016 年 8 月

Brief Chronicle of Bubbles

The burning world scorches me like cinders
Yet cedes me a small patch of shade to cool myself
I have never been an ascetic like Weil and Sengcan
Healing humanity's fragmentation
I have no appetite for boiling sand into rice
Nor the courage to slice my flesh to feed tigers
I was born by a breezy, verdant riverbank
Line after line of bubbles
Knocking on my door
I know that this unbroken chain of death
Must make way for this rupture of a race
The river at twilight, a swirling liaison
I watch the boundless frothing
And at the moment before bursting and returning to water
Is a mysterious force without a name
As if a monster of the mind is
helplessly hiding within
I know how to link each rupture of language and will
  and make
Them dance—
This is my life's work

I must cherish it like ants
My skyscraper is being erected on a foundation of
empty bubbles

August 2016

崖邊口占

閑看驚雀何如？
凌厲古調難彈。
斧斫老松何如？
斷口正是我的冠冕

懸崖何時來到我的體內又
何時離去
山水有尚未被獵取的憨直
餘輝久積而為琥珀
從絕壁攀援而下的女遊客
一身好聞的
青木瓜之味

2016 年 8 月

Cliffside Account

Idling, I wonder at the startled sparrow.
These high-spirited ancient tunes are the hardest to play.
What of the axe hewing the hoary pine?
The cleaving point is also my coronet.

When did the precipice arrive within my body and
When did it depart
The landscape has an honesty that knows no hunters
The afterglow congeals into amber
And slowly descending the sheer cliff, a lady tourist
Is perfumed by the scent
Of unripe papayas

August 2016

枯樹賦

上山時看見一株巨大枯樹
橫臥路側
被雷擊過又似被完整地剝了皮
烏黑暗啞地泛著光
我猜偷伐者定然寢食不安
但二十人合圍也不能盡攬入懷的
樹幹令他們畏而止步

在滿目青翠中這種
不顧一切的死，確實太醒目了

像一個人大睜著眼睛坐在
無邊無際的盲者中間
他該説些甚麼

倘以此獨死為獨活呢
萬木皆因忍受而蔥蘢
我們也可以一身蒼翠地死去

我們也可用時代的滿目瘡痍加上

這棵枯樹再構出謝朓的心跳
而忘了有一種拒絕從
他空空的名字秘密地遺傳至今

2016年8月

Ode to a Withered Tree

Climbing the mountain I spot a big dead tree
Horizontal on the road
It must have been struck by lightning, its bark all peeled
Dark and dull yet emitting a certain shine
I imagine those who secretly felled it unable to eat or sleep
This trunk twenty people holding hands couldn't encompass
Must have inhibited the thieves and caused them to stop

To die amidst all this luxuriant green
Abandoning everything: what a smart move

Like a person, eyes wide open, sitting
Amongst countless blind people
What should he say?

If because of this, we take dying alone as living alone
All nature will bud and burgeon because of the bearing
And so we can also pass away into the verdant foliage

We can also add to this age's wounds, found everywhere
The resurrected heartbeat of this decaying tree

And forget that a kind of rejection
Derives from an empty name being secretly passed on
  to the present

August 2016

街頭即繪

那令槐花開放的
也必令梨花開放

讓一個盲丐止步的
卻絕不會讓一個警察止步

道一聲精準多麼難
雖然盲丐
在街頭
會遭遇太多的蔑稱
而警察在這個國度，卻擁有
深淵般的權力

他們寂靜而
醒目
在灰濛濛的街道之間

正午
花香湧向何處不可知
懸崖將崩於誰手不可知

2016 年3 月

Improvised Street Painting

What makes pagodatree flowers blossom
Also makes pear flowers blossom

But what stays the steps of a blind beggar
Will never stop a policeman

How difficult it is to be precise
Although a blind beggar
On the street
will be scorned
The police in this country possess
Boundless power

They are silent
And smart
On these grey bleak streets

Noon
We know not where the flowers' fragrance blows
Nor do we know in whose hands the precipice shall crumble

March 2016

渺茫的本體

每一個緘默物體等著我們
剝離出幽閉其中的呼救聲
湖水說不
遂有漣漪
這遠非一個假設：當我
跑步至湖邊
湖水剛剛形成
當我攀至山頂，在磨得
皮開肉綻的鞋底
六和塔剛剛建成
在塔頂閑坐了幾分鐘
直射的光線讓人恍惚
這恍惚不可說
這一眼望去的水濁舟孤不可說
這一身遲來的大汗不可說
這芭蕉葉上的
漫長空白不可說
我的出現
像寧靜江面突然伸出一隻手
搖幾下就

永遠地消失了
這只手不可說
這由即興物象強制壓縮而成的
詩的身體不可說
一切語言盡可廢去，在
語言的無限彈性把我的
無數具身體從這一瞬間打撈出來的
生死兩茫茫不可說

2016年3月

The Unspeakable Body

Every silent object awaits us
Peeling itself from entrapped screams
The lakewater says no
Followed by the ripples
This is far more than an assumption: When I
Ran to the lake shore
Its water had just formed
When I climbed to the mountaintop, under the
Soles of my shoes that were completely torn
Liuhe Pagoda had just been built
Sitting idle on its top for a while
The light piercing the structure put me in a trance
A trance that's unspeakable
This lone boat on the turbid water is unspeakable
This latent body of sweat is unspeakable
The long emptiness
Above the banana leaves is unspeakable
My appearance
Is like a hand reaching out of a glass lake
Waving a few times

And disappearing forever
This hand cannot speak
These forcefully compressed improvisations of
Poems' bodies do not say
All languages are obsolete—in
The infinite elasticity of the language let my
Countless bodies be salvaged in this instant
From between life and death's unspeakable shores

March 2016

歲聿其逝

防波堤上一棵柳樹
陷在數不清的柳樹之中
繞湖跑步的女孩
正一棵棵穿過
她跑得太快了
一次次衝破自己的軀殼
而湖上
白鷺很慢
在女孩與白鷺的裂隙裏
下夜班的護士正走下
紅色出租車
一年將盡
白鷺取走它在世間的一切
緊貼著水面正安靜地離去

2016年1月

A Year in Passing

A willow on the jetty
Is trapped among countless others
The girl jogging around the lake
Past the willows one by one
Running too fast
She bursts through her body again and again
Yet on the lake
The egret is slow
Between the girl and the egret
A nurse getting off her night shift is stepping out of
A red taxi
The year is drawing to a close
The egret takes with it all that the world can offer
And glides quietly away, skimming the water

January 2016

不可多得的容器

我書房中的容器
都是空的
幾個小缽，以前種過水仙花
有過璀璨片刻
但它們統統被清空了
我在書房不捨晝夜的寫作
跟這種空
有甚麼樣關係？
精研眼前的事物和那
不可見的恆河水
總是貌似刁鑽、晦澀——
難以作答。
我的寫作和這窗縫中逼過來的
碧雲天，有甚麼樣關係？
多數時刻
我一無所繫地抵案而眠

2016年1月

Rare Containers

The containers in my library
Are all empty
Several small pots had been for daffodils
Which had blossomed for a while
But they are all emptied out
I write day and night in this library
What is the relationship between me
And this emptiness?
My careful study of the things before me and
that Ganges River, cannot be seen,
always seem difficult, obscure—
difficult to answer.
And what is the relationship between my writing
And the blue sky squeezed through the crevices of the windows?
Occasionally
leaning on the desk, associated with nothing, I sleep

January 2016

深嗅

油菜花伏地而黃
有人佇立
不語
這個時代灌注給一個旁觀者的
厭倦有多深
取決於這種最熟悉的花在我
每一側面的崩潰
還將持續多久

轉眼即見破碎如同我
無法統一自己
反過來的結論也成立嗎？
「無為」二字在雨中閃光
葛洪醫生，
請修補我！

這花瓣會交出一個新的入口？
當我和我體內的
廢墟
深深地

嗅著它
我體內的蓬頭垢面嗅著它
我身上每一種失敗
湧回來
從器官的無數缺口中
嗅著它
畢生在泥土中奔命卻從未深俯於
一朵花的老媽媽
懷揣著遠未出生的我
也奮不顧身前來
嗅著它

2016 年3 月

Deep Sniffing

Rapeseed flowers bow yellow
Someone is standing there
Mute
How profound
The sense of fatigue the age gives the spectator
Depends on the collapsing
Of this flower I know best on every side of me.
How long can it last?

A blink of an eye and all is shattered, as if I
Cannot keep myself together
Does this conclusion still hold in reverse?
The word “inaction” glitters in the rain
Dr Ge Hong
Please fix me!

Do these petals present a new entry?
When I and the ruins
Inside me
Sniff them
Deeply

Everything that is unkempt inside me sniffing them
The failures on my body
Rush back
From the countless organ wounds
Sniffing them
A lifetime of soil-bound toil yet I never lowered my head
The old mother of a flower
Is speculating about an unborn me
dashing forward, with abandon
To sniffs them

March 2016

在永失中

我沿鋥亮的直線由皖入川
一路上閉著眼，聽粗大雨點
砸著窗玻璃的重力，和時光
在鋼鐵中緩緩擴散的漣漪
此時此器無以言傳
彷彿仍在我超穩定結構的書房裏
聽著夜間鳥鳴從四壁
一絲絲滲透進來
這一聲和那一聲
之間，恍惚隔著無數個世紀
想想李白當年，由川入皖穿透的
是峭壁猿鳴和江面的漩渦
而此刻，狀如槍膛的高鐵在
隧洞裏隨我撲入一個接
一個明滅多變的時空
時速六百里足以讓蝴蝶的孤獨
退回一隻繭的孤獨
這一路我丟失牆壁無限
我丟失的鳥鳴從皖南幻影般小山隼
到蜀道艱深的白頭翁

這些年我最痛苦的一次喪失是
在五道口一條陋巷裏
我看見那個我從椅子上站起來了
慢慢走過來了
兩個人臉挨臉坐著
在兩個容器裏。窗玻璃這邊我
打著盹。那邊的我在明暗
不定風馳電掣的丟失中

2016年5月

In Eternal Loss

I follow the gleaming line from Anhui into Sichuan
Eyes closed the whole time, listening to thick raindrops
Hammering on the windows, and time
Rippling in the steel, a slow dispersion
This time, this moment, I am speechless
As though I am still in my strongly built study
Listening to birdsong seeping
Through the walls
Between this sound and
that sound, as though countless centuries have passed
Think of Li Bai that year, travelling from Sichuan to Anhui amidst
The cries of gibbons on the cliff and the ripples on the lake
And this moment, the train like the chamber of a gun
Follows me through the tunnel and leaps into
coruscating dimension after coruscating dimension
Six hundred miles an hour, quick enough for the butterfly's loneliness
To regress into the loneliness of a caterpillar
On this journey I have lost walls beyond measure

My missing birdcalls issue from South Anhui's mirage-
  like hills
To a white-haired poet on the treacherous road to Sichuan
All these years my most painful loss
Was on a mean ugly alley in Wudaokou
I see that other me stand up from the chair
And slowly walk over
The two of us seated, our faces touching
In two containers. On this side of the window I
Am dozing off, while the other me is
lost in the flashing light of the night

May 2016

膝上牡丹花

年輕的值班醫生對我耳語
燈下那個女人體內
胎兒早已死去
她在牡丹花布下拱起的腹部已是
一座孤墳

她輕嚼口香糖，出神盯著
簾後穿窗的飛鳥
夕光在窗玻璃上正冷卻
醫生想寫下幾句
提著筆又沉吟不定

我也曾是一座孤墳壓在
母親腰間
那令我活下來的到底是些甚麼
年年膝上花開，細雨中
牡丹的容顏難以言盡
今年三月，我手提鋥亮的大砍刀上山
把老父墳前草木砍了個乾乾淨淨

必須寫下幾句來
分擔此刻的緘默
嗆人的青草和黏土味
即便到了我們這個年紀
即便牡丹的根在那些洗白了並
永不再穿上的布衣中
已扎得那麼深

2015年9月

The Peonies on the Knees

The young doctor on duty whispers to me
The fetus in the woman under the light
Is dead
That dome-shaped belly under the cover with peony prints
Is now an orphan's tomb

Chewing gum, she stares at
The birds outside the window
The sunset light on the glass is cooling down
The doctor wants to write down a few sentences
He raises the pen but hesitates

I was also once in an orphan's tomb
Resting on my mother's waist
What was it that let me live?
Year by year flowers open on her knees, amidst the drizzle
the faces of the peonies are hard to describe
This March, I climbed the mountain with a gleaming machete
And chopped down the grass and trees before my father's grave

I must write down a few sentences
To lessen the burden of this silence
And the choking smell of new grass and clay
Even at my age
Even if those garments are bleached and
Will never be worn again, how deep reach
The roots of those peonies

September 2015

陳先發（中國大陸），安徽桐城人。1989年畢業於復旦大學。著有詩集《春天的死亡之書》（1994）、《前世》（2005）、長篇小説《拉魂腔》（2006）、詩集《寫碑之心》（2011）、隨筆集《黑池壩筆記》（2014）、詩集《養鶴問題》（2015，台灣版）、《裂隙與巨眼》（2016）等。曾獲獎項有「十月詩歌獎」、「十月文學獎」、「1986–2006年中國十大新鋭詩人」、「2008年中國年度詩人」、「1998年至2008年中國十大影響力詩人」、「首屆中國海南詩歌雙年獎」、「首屆袁可嘉詩歌獎」、「天問詩歌獎」、「中國桂冠詩歌獎」、「2015年桃花潭國際詩會中國傑出詩人獎」、「陳子昂詩歌獎」、「安徽文學獎」等數十種。2015年與北島等十位詩人一起獲得中華書局等機構聯合評選的「新詩貢獻獎」。作品被譯成英、法、俄、西班牙、希臘等多種文字傳播。

Chen Xianfa (Mainland China) was born in 1967 in Anhui and graduated from Fudan University in Shanghai in 1989. He has published several books of poetry, including *Death in Springtime* (1994), *A Past Life* (2005), *The Heart of Writing Steles* (2011), *The Problem of Raising Cranes* (Taiwan, 2015), and *Crevice and Insight* (2016), as well as the novel *Soul-Stealing Opera* (2006) and the essays *Notes on Black Pond Dam* (2014). He has received well over a dozen domestic poetry prizes, including the October Poetry Prize, the 2008 Poet of the Year Award, and Fudan University's Award for Literary Achievement. His works have been translated into English, French, Russian, Spanish, and Greek.

香港國際詩歌之夜 2017
International Poetry Nights in Hong Kong 2017

主辦單位 Organizers

香港中文大學文學院
Faculty of Arts, The Chinese University of Hong Kong
香港詩歌節基金會有限公司
Hong Kong Poetry Festival Foundation Limited

協辦單位 Co-organizers

香港中文大學中國文化研究所
Institute of Chinese Studies, The Chinese University of Hong Kong
香港中文大學出版社
The Chinese University Press
香港大學美術博物館
The University Museum and Art Gallery, The University of Hong Kong
香港大學文學院
Faculty of Arts, The University of Hong Kong
香港科技大學賽馬會高等研究院
Jockey Club Institute for Advanced Study, Hong Kong University of Science and Technology
香港科技大學人文學部
Division of Humanities, Hong Kong University of Science and Technology
廣州時刻文化傳播有限公司
Moment Communications
活字文化
MoveableType Legacy (Beijing) Co., Ltd.
當當
DANGDANG

贊助 Sponsors

中國會 The China Club
北京匡時國際拍賣有限公司 Beijing Council International Auction Co., Ltd.
先鋒公益基金會 UCF Charity Foundation Limited
卓爾書店 the zall bookstore
斑馬谷文化發展有限公司 Zebra Valley Culture Development
馮鑫牟希文夫婦 Feng Xin (Larry) and Mu Xi Wen (Maggie)
蓮華書院 Lianhua Academy